70p

PERFECT E-COMMERCE

1

PERFECT E-COMMERCE

All you need to get it right first time

Steve Morris and
Paul Dickinson

1 3 5 7 9 10 8 6 4 2

This edition published in the United Kingdom in 2000
by Random House Business Books

First published in 2000 by Random House Business Books,
Random House, 20 Vauxhall Bridge Road, London SW1V 2SA

Random House Australia (Pty) Limited
20 Alfred Street, Milsons Point
Sydney, New South Wales 2061, Australia

Random House New Zealand Limited
18 Poland Road, Glenfield
Auckland 10, New Zealand

Random House (Pty) Limited
Endulini, 5a Jubilee Road, Parktown 2193, South Africa

The Random House Group Limited Reg. No. 954009

Papers used by Random House are natural, recyclable
products made from wood grown in sustainable forests. The
manufacturing processes conform to the environmental regulations
of the country of origin.

ISBN 0 09 9401582 8

Companies, institutions and other organizations wishing to make
bulk purchases of any business books published by Random House
should contact their local bookstore or Random House direct:
Special Sales Director
Random House, 20 Vauxhall Bridge Road, London SW1V 2SA

Tel: 020 7840 8470 Fax: 020 7828 6681

www.randomhouse.co.uk
businessbooks@randomhouse.co.uk

Typeset in Sabon by SX Composing DTP, Rayleigh, Essex
Printed and bound in Great Britain by Cox & Wyman Ltd, Reading

Contents

CHAPTER 1

Understanding the power of the web

In 1988 the typewriter entered into a period of terminal demise. It was killed by the personal computer, or PC. Over the next four years PCs killed filing clerks, typists, carbon paper and a host of other seemingly essential office traditions. But this was only the beginning of the beginning of a process that may never end. We will soon see the end of the office memo, killed by the informal e-mail. Interestingly we are also seeing a related death, with the formal office suit and tie being replaced with freedom of dress. When the uniforms change you know you have a revolution on your hands.

Like most revolutions, at the very start it was not apparent what was happening. Many people in the design industry scoffed at the idea that these little boxes could replace the ancient art of typing. But then computers became networked. The paper memo died, we began to gain easy access to each other's files, and electronic searching for documents emerged, all of it a technology that could double productivity instantly. When in 1995 the Internet arrived, almost everything in business changed for ever.

In the mid 1990s it was fashionable to scoff at the 'world wide wait'. This slur still has some validity today but in the ensuing years events of far more importance have emerged to alter the environment beyond recognition.

An Internet bookshop, barely five years old, has come to be worth at its peak more that $28 billion. Directors of transnational companies have lost their jobs because they failed to grasp what was happening. No organization is immune to the changes in train. There are many fascinating stories from Silicon Valley regarding the land grab for users, with free e-mail as the spur. Next came a European revolution built on free Internet access as Freeserve, and a host of imitators emerged to snap up customers.

Despite the appearance of strange new companies such as Yahoo! and dictionary.com, with obscure and difficult-to-fathom revenue models, there is one inexorable trend that defines what has been happening to the Internet since 1995; an increasing focus on money. E-commerce is the end game of the Internet. The predictions that e-commerce could reach $10 billion or more by 2003 have all now been forgotten; forecasters now talk of one *trillion* dollars or more next year, perhaps this year. We live in a unique age. True to the Chinese curse, 'may you live in interesting times' these are indeed interesting times.

When we wrote a book about web sites in 1998 Dell computers were selling $1 million of goods each day from their site. By the time the book was published, the figure had risen to $10 million each day. Now it is more than $30 million each day. World wide, McDonalds have 27,000 restaurants; the Dell.com web site takes more money each day than all of them combined. There is definitely something in this e-commerce business!

At the time of writing, mid 2000, business-to-business e-commerce has emerged as the dominant phenomenon. Each week vast companies in industries such as chemicals, aerospace, motors and construction announce e-commerce market places elevating the traditional concept of EDI (Electronic Data Interchange) with suppliers into a fast, fluid market-place with low cost of access. Far sooner than anyone anticipated, Internet traffic has exceeded voice traffic on telecommunications networks.

This striking development raises serious issues for telecommunications companies. Unsurprisingly, the big question is, who will pay for communications? Currently data traffic provides only a fraction of the revenue from voice. So at just the time when network operators are compelled to make huge investments, revenue is falling dramatically. Of course mobile is booming, but perhaps somewhat apart from the main networks.

Revenues will be generated, and they will come from e-commerce. In a few years, today's bold efforts in e-commerce, exemplified by Amazon, Ebay and Egg, will be dwarfed . . . by, perhaps, your next move?

HOW THE INTERNET WORKS

Technology fans will be familiar with the story of the Internet's development, and how it has grown. But for the uninitiated, a quick summary. The Internet was developed by the Pentagon some twenty years ago with a single objective, namely, to facilitate communications in the event of a nuclear war. In essence, it defines routes for data communications on an ad hoc basis, so that if half the system was blown up, the other half would still work. To compare the Internet and the telephone system:

	TELEPHONE	INTERNET
Data	Sent in sequence	Broken into 'packets'
Routing	Point-to-Point Exchange	Any route available

In summary, the Internet offers a means to enjoy economies of scale in communications. To use a crude analogy; each telephone connection uses up the telecoms equivalent of a single lane from the beginning of its journey right through to the end, for every second of the call; in contrast Internet traffic breaks data streams into packets. Suddenly, instead of one car in each lane, a million cars can use a motorway, simultaneously.

The World Wide Web

It has been said that you have to get up early in the morning to spot the difference between the Internet and the World Wide Web. Developed originally by Tim Berners-Lee at the CERN particle physics laboratory, the web is essentially a Graphic User Interface (GUI) for the data exchange on the Internet. It allows users to click on underlined text, or connected graphics to jump from location to location. The programming language of the web is Hyper Text Mark-up Language or HTML. For mobile devices a similar software language is used called Wireless Mark-up Language or WML.

The device that allows users to jump seamlessly from location to location is called a 'browser'. The first popular browser, Mosaic, was followed by the very popular Navigator, made available free by Netscape. A lot of Internet software has been free ever since, setting demanding expectations for service providers.

Browsers have continued to develop functionality including frames, Java and a host of other functions. Deploying your e-commerce functionality to match the capabilities of the great mass of browsers is key. Boo.com famously over-specified their technology and failed in this area.

What the Internet means for business

The new communications architecture has many practical consequences for business. The migration to broadband media is a permanent one and this in turn will simply increase the potential of the web for business. We are going to see:

- Rapidly increasing speed of connection
- Improving quality of service
- Falling prices
- Greater uptake
- Global adoption
- Emerging standards
- Big winners
- Numerous new entrants.

To summarize, electronic media are becoming instrumental to the way we communicate and consume goods and services. In many respects, the so-called TMT, or Technology, Media and Telecommunications sectors, are replacing physical goods as the most important sector in the economy. To give an example, for more than twenty years the percentage of disposable income spent on cars has been in steady decline. Conversely, the percentage spent on mobile telephony has been rising dramatically over just five years.

These statistics have positive implications. New media means the death of distance. The carbon fuelled economy will dwindle in significance. Information will triumph. The auction of third generation UK mobile licences for £22 billion is partial proof of this trend.

There can be no doubt that information technology has transformed our world. To try and build a more useful picture of how the new media work, and to explain the components of e-commerce, let's look at some of the core principles.

To begin with some jargon, the world's e-commerce markets are divided into rudimentary categories, and they have simple acronyms to describe them.

B2C stands for 'Business to Consumers'. In other words, when a company uses e-commerce to service consumers directly, like Amazon.com, yahoo.com and egg.com.

As a general rule, when dealing with established brands, consumers feel comfortable handing over their credit card details. Over two million people have purchased books by credit card with Amazon. It has not been easy of course, coping with such demand. Senior managers of Amazon are famed for holding weekly meetings to predict which system will be overpowered next. But as a general rule, if your brand is known, people will buy by credit card or debit card.

B2B stands for 'Business to Business' and it has emerged as one of the areas of most interest on the web. Examples include Cisco.com, MySAP.com and Oracle.com. In B2B, companies trade directly with other companies. This is easy to organize, and as most settlements are conducted via invoices, there is less requirement for immediate automated cash transferred settlement.

Forrester Research estimates that business-to-business e-commerce will grow from $109 billion in 1999 to $2.7 trillion in 2004. GartnerGroup puts the figure closer to $7 trillion in 2004. Big stuff.

B2E stands for 'Business to Employee'. B2E web sites are generally held on intranets and their objective is to sell a company's own goods or services to employees.

There are still more permutations of these acronyms developing, such B2G for 'Business to Government', G2C, 'Government to Consumer', and many others.

B2C is very different from all previous forms of commerce, although there are perhaps some precedents in living memory. While our grandparents were used to giving a shopping order over the phone, today we are using computers to bypass the cost and effort of the shop assistant taking orders. Further – and this is perhaps the greatest asset of e-commerce – we can now shop for anything, anywhere in the world, without leaving the house.

What makes an e-commerce site special
- Open 24 hours a day, seven days a week, all year (known as 24/7 service)
- Completely up to date, at 300 million PCs
- Available in every country in the world
- Theoretically requires zero staff
- Capable of interactivity.

Interactivity opens a window to an amazing present and a dramatic future. Interactivity permits the seller and buyer to communicate, anytime, any place, anywhere. When they communicate they can:

Show photos of goods
Describe services
Allow users to view goods in any amount of detail
Offer unlimited information and images
Easily compare with competitors

Search electronically, almost instantly, through millions of products and data

Calculate instantly cost permutations, exchange rates, postage and packaging etc.

Check availability

Take money

Communicate an order directly to a manufacturer

Communicate the same order to manufacturing suppliers

Offer unlimited information about your company

Provide an electronic forum for consumers to discuss your products with each other

Watch short videos of goods and services

Hear music, voices or both

Download applications like calculators, screensavers or documentation to aid sales support

Check credit status online

Plan complicated holidays with real-time live calculation of variables and checking availability

Offer live events like auctions, or news as it breaks

Provide whole books to download electronically

Instigate telephone calls directly from web sites

Offer real-time checking on the status of orders and delivery

Provide links to related web sites

Change the content depending on the customer enquiry

Leave a 'cookie' on the user's computer to allow identification during future visits

Build up a data profile of users

Offer services like so-called 'strictly applications' that make them return to your site, such as a free, branded web diary

And that's not all. Perhaps the most important

developments in e-commerce are being developed right now by many tens of thousands of entrepreneurs and programmers (developers) in Silicon Valley, Stockholm and Bangalore.

What Businesses move to the Web? Which are born there?

One of the most famous of all e-commerce entrepreneurs is Jeff Bezos, founder of Amazon.com. He had never run a shop, but he realized ahead of others that the Internet was going to be the biggest shop in the world. He chose the name Amazon because it was short, easy to remember and conjured up the image of a great, powerful flow. That was what he wanted his business to achieve.

To get to the heart of the computer revolution, like the thousands of entrepreneurs who have followed, Bezos went to the west coast of USA, home to the mighty Microsoft, Intel, Oracle and Cisco, as well as numerous smaller businesses that fill the gaps in the blossoming information architecture. On the way he planned to build the biggest e-commerce business in the world. Although he always planned for Amazon to sell more than one line, he knew the opportunity to make a name would be optimized if he concentrated on just one area. He knew computers well, and was looking for an e-commerce opportunity that would make the best use of information technology.

Out of the twenty product categories that were shortlisted he chose, quite brilliantly, books. His thinking was that because there were more than two million titles on sale, finding any one of them was very difficult indeed. But he also knew a good computer could search a database of two million entries in a second or two. He figured, correctly, that if he could offer the utility of a book search engine at a web site, many orders would be forthcoming.

Clearly, the development of Amazon.com was not dependent on the success of an existing business. Amazon benefited from what is called 'first mover advantage'. This is a process of acquiring significant brand recognition through easy PR. Conversely, Bertelsmann, the giant German publishing company, ignored the web, at least at first. But as a year or two passed by, it became clear that Amazon was here to stay. They could ignore the power of e-commerce no longer. Now Bertelsmann is constantly enlarging its commitment to the web, focusing on the bookselling site Bol.com.

These two stories show that if a web site is worth doing by a start-up new business, it is worth doing by an established company. E-commerce respects no boundaries, and it is democratic in effect. To the computer users, the Harrods web site is the same size on screen as your local corner shop. And if the corner shop site works better, and can attract traffic to the site, it may get more business. To summarize the situations for both parties:

New web sites (start-ups)

Advantages
Unafraid to cannibalize existing business (they have none)
No pre-conceived notions
Web 'savvy'
Global mindset
Able to offer stock options
Low barriers to entry

Disadvantages
Zero brand recognition
Very limited funds
Inexperienced management
No logistics infrastructure
Low barriers to entry

For established businesses moving to the web

Advantages
Established brand
Financial clout
Organizational capability
Existing infrastructure

Disadvantages
Fear of cannibalizing conventional business
Limited vision
Unable to offer significant stock options
Substantial overhead

These are still early days in the fight between new and old businesses. The opportunities for new entrants are huge. But the old 'bricks and mortar' businesses are fast becoming 'clicks and mortar'.

Some Ingredients of Success, and Failure
In the UK there is one outstanding example of an established business using the power of the web to achieve something spectacular. Dixons Group plc, owners of the eponymous electrical stores, as well as PC World, Curry's and The Link, conceived a brilliant business plan in 1998 for the free Internet service provider 'Freeserve'.

Having identified a gap in the market for such a

service, it was necessary to seize the opportunity on a large scale, because other companies would no doubt come in quickly to imitate, as some 200 have subsequently done. With a budget of several million, and meticulous planning, the service was launched, with free CDs available in all Dixons stores. National advertising and brilliant merchandising took Freeserve to more than a million users in a few months, so that from a tiny investment a business worth some £8 billion was created. At the stock market peak, Freeserve had a market capitalization that looked set to eclipse the rest of Dixons Group itself.

A spectacular web failure is Boo.com. Armed with nothing more substantial than an idea to sell sportswear over the Internet, a group of entrepreneurs raised significant venture capital. They built a formidable staff of 400 but delivered what many considered to be an over complicated web site. People were directed to the site by rather oblique advertising. The result was insufficient customers, excessive running costs (known as burn rate), and an inadequate consumer proposition.

Above all, the lack of customers was obviously key. The advertising guru Winston Fletcher has observed that most start-up dot.com businesses will fail because they simply cannot afford the advertising required to build the brand. Of course some brilliant innovators such as Yahoo!, Amazon, Hotmail and ICQ have built powerful global brands through word of mouth alone, so-called 'viral marketing', but these are exceptions, built on first-to-market, functional excellence and scalable technology.

Winston Fletcher's observation is that some of the world's biggest advertisers like Proctor and Gamble already have well-established brands, yet they continue to advertise heavily just to maintain brand recognition. This is, crucially, what most of the upstart 'dot coms' cannot afford to do. So people will forget their names, nobody will visit, they will go bust, as Boo.com has done.

So why do some e-commerce ventures succeeed and others fail? It's a hard one to answer. But it is true that successful ventures tend to start with a great idea, sensible planning and rely on good partners.

Revolutions often begin as ideas. Sometimes they stem from an invention (the printing press), or from a concept (think of the impact 'freedom' has had on revolutions in the past). The Internet is no exception. Even though its original *raison d'etre* was the functional one of providing for security in the event of a nuclear attack, it quickly escaped its genesis to become a powerful ideological symbol. Nowadays, it is clear that the defence priorities of governments were relatively unimportant. What really consolidated the Internet as a popular medium was the zeal and commitment of thousands of unknown individuals who quickly grasped its possibilities for the development of world-wide communication.

The Potential for New Forms of Marketing and Advertising

The Internet is a peculiar place. Everything is just one click away from everything else. Each banner advert is a doorway to that whole site. In essence people can be in and out of your shop in seconds. Increasing evidence suggests that banner adverts simply do not work. Others argue that they will evolve an intelligence based on data analysis and come to act more as an assistant than an advert.

There are several significant components to web marketing including:

- Choosing or buying the right URL (Universal Resource Locator, the web site address)
- Optimizing relationships with search engines
- Meta file headings
- Reciprocal links
- Encouraging 'stickiness'
- Mass personalization
- Encouraging self-provisions of content

URLs

There can only be one dictionary.com, only one oil.com, one Ford.com. Many web users looking for something may try and guess the URL first. If you want IBM, chances are you will find them at IBM.com. Amazon is a great name for a different reason. Obvious URLs such as money.com and finance.com were registered long ago by shrewd people, and can be sold for millions of dollars.

Optimizing relationships with search engines/meta file headings

Search engines regularly scan the web recording data from every single web site, usually the first hundred words, the so called Meta File headings. This database is then 'searched' every time someone enters a search word or words. There are four main ways to rise up the search engines:

1. Formally register with search engines

It is possible to register your web site with search engines. Take trouble to understand and fit in with their data structure.

2. Develop smart 'meta file' headings

Search engines usually search only the first fifty words your prospective customers will see. For example if you sell unique military flags, include those words in the first fifty on your site, in as many different forms as possible. But do not simply duplicate endlessly, as search engines use de-duplication technology to avoid falling for this trick. However, if you are a bank, it may be more difficult to stand out.

3. Buy search results

Some search engines sell the results of searches for a fee. If you want to get found you may have to pay! Better still, you can be featured on a search engine. The web diary company eCal paid $12 million to be offered on the service of Lycos, the Internet search engine.

4. Create multiple home pages

One odd, but clever, way to rise up the search engines is to create five, fifty, perhaps five hundred home pages. In this way you can rise up the search ratings. But it is cheating in a certain sense. At least it can reduce the quality of other people's searches. But that is typical of the Internet. Lawless and without any set protocols.

Reciprocal Links

The art of Internet commerce relates to maximizing the flow of traffic, or users, to your site. Spending billions of dollars developing your web presence will prove pointless if nobody visits the site. Harking back to the good old amateur days of the Internet, when it was a hobbyist medium, the tradition of supplying links provides a simple means to increase your web exposure. To pursue this route consider all the most appropriate links to have on your site. For example, if you run a guest house in Brighton, you might want links to web sites showing what's on in the town, perhaps a coach company, a sailing boat hire company, etc. Next, contact all these sites saying you want to put a link to their site on yours, and ask if you can have one on theirs. The fashionable concept of a portal is a notable extension of this process.

Portals

Nobody is quite sure what the exact meaning of the word 'portal' actually is. However, few would dispute that Yahoo.com, the world's most visited web site, is a successful portal. When you look at Yahoo! you can see they have tried to combine in one place everything you could ever want. If a portal does a good job of compiling content, you have no reason to leave. And you will keep coming back. Other good examples of portals are FT.com, BT.com and BBC.co.uk. In their different ways they give people what they want, to make them stay.

Encouraging 'Stickiness'

If you run a shop it is obviously desirable to have return visits and repeat business. The same applies to e-commerce sites. A sticky application is one that encourages users to revisit your site repeatedly.

Mass personalization

E-commerce and Internet are driven by increasing computing power and database capabilities. As mentioned earlier, these systems can manage huge amounts of information. This raises a series of interesting retail possibilities. Rather than describe the technology in detail, it may be simpler to list a series of possible web site messages that you might encounter on a web site today.

'Hi Steve Morris, welcome back to XYZ.com'
'You searched for "fishing". Would you like to see what we have under the category Angling?'
'You bought a book about fly fishing last week, do you want to:
   1. See what others have said about the book?

2. Tell others what you think about it?

3. See other books by the same author?

4. See other material about fly fishing?

5. Contact other people who have read the book?

'We hope you are finding the XYZ.com Anglers diary useful. Do you want to see where other anglers in the area are fishing?'

'Fly fishing is particularly popular in five areas within one hour's drive of your house, would you like to see where?'

'You booked the four star Grange Hotel by Lake Wyndemere last August. Do you want to see other hotels of the same quality near other popular fishing areas?'

The above examples are simple. More complex offers can be achieved. As computer consultant Graham Barratt has stated, 'If you can think it, you can do it.'

Encouraging Self-Provision of Content

The greatest power of the Internet is as a tool for information aggregation and exchange. Following on from some of the principles of mass personalization comes self-provisioning, which in some respects is the most powerful process available on the web for creating value.

At the heart of self-provisioning are two concepts. One is for the user or consumer to grasp, the other is for the commercial web entrepreneur.

The consumer principle of self-provisioning can be summarized as 'The more information you provide the network, the more utility it will give you.'

In essence this means that all suppliers of tailored e-commerce will benefit from acquiring the most accurate possible profile of your needs and wishes. Like a good personal assistant, intelligent e-commerce sites will want to know as much about you as possible. In exchange for access to your personal 'profile', which may become very extensive over time, e-commerce sites will be able to offer dramatically relevant offers. This thinking is part of the background to the outlandish valuation of Internet service providers in so far as ISPs can know every web site you have visited.

Subject to the development of a more liberal legal regime for data protection, banking records may also serve as key data sets to develop evolved web advertising and deal broking.

Web business applications of self-provisioning have a simple core principle. If one person maintains your web site, it will have a value. If ten people are paid to do so, it will have more. Can you afford to pay one hundred people to maintain your web site? Almost certainly not, even though it might seem like a nice idea.

But what if a thousand people, ten thousand or even a million people, were to add their contribution to your web site? What if they did this hourly, daily, weekly, night and day, all year round? And what if they did this completely free of charge, from all over the world?

That is the business model of some of the most spectacular web businesses. Auction sites such as ebay.com and QXL.com, homepage sites such as Tripod.com and Geocities.com, diary sites such as diarymanager.com and eCal.com, all prove the fidelity and strength of the self-provisioning model. Amazon.com contains book reviews sent in by customers, the BT service www.getoutthere.bt.com contains music uploaded to the web by aspiring pop stars. Dating and employment agencies such as DatingDirect.com and Eurojobs.com leverage the benefit of many users. All the while this process builds value for the web site owner!

To summarize, self-provisioning is a mechanism whereby what would be better kept on the Internet is put there by people of their own volition; and whereby an Internet entrepreneur finds both an attractive way to package the service and a channel for viral marketing to make user numbers snowball.

Overall, the objective is to create a circle wherein visitors to your site deposit information that attracts more visitors to your site, and they deposit more information that attracts more visitors who in turn deposit more information. This process will, over time, prove instrumental in our optimization of the Internet's extraordinary potential.

VIRTUAL FULFILMENT MECHANISMS THAT WORK

To simplify an examination of fulfilment logistics we can split goods into two basic categories, namely material and dematerialized.

Material goods are anything that needs to be delivered to your home; food, clothes, drink, flowers, durable goods, etc.

Dematerialized goods and services embrace financial services, air tickets, music downloads, online education, erotic material, education and training, web magazines and newspapers, etc.

The key point about fulfilment mechanisms is that only material goods have any excuse for problems. Dematerialized goods should just arrive. To give an example, Tesco in the UK deliver food to thousands of households each week. The order fulfilment is sometimes wrong, but regular users tolerate the occasional error to enjoy the fantastic utility of not having to visit the shop physically.

Establishing logistics that really work is a perpetual challenge. A former senior manager at Cable & Wireless UK, years ago suggested acquiring Unigate, the dairy and delivery company, just to get hold of their van fleet. Powerful national retailers such as the John Lewis Partnership have been slow to put their van fleets to work in the most difficult aspect of e-commerce, namely fulfilment. Part of the attraction for Great Universal Stores (GUS) at the time of their first major venture into e-commerce was ownership of their White Arrow van delivery service, a home delivery capability greater than Parcelforce.

To try and grasp the scale and importance of the challenge to deliver physical goods effectively in e-commerce fulfilment, it is instructive to look at the recent career move of George Shaheen, formerly chief executive of Andersen Consulting, the world's largest management consultancy, with 65,000 employees and $9 billion turnover. He gave up that job to join web-van.com, a tiny internet start-up that is projected to make a loss this year of $73m on sales of $11.9m.

As described above there are many different products and services that can be delivered completely online. For these categories, the simple rule is that consumers will expect something not far off a 100 per cent fault-free service. Naturally the web's reputation for somewhat patchy service may provide a mitigating circumstance that forgives errors. But the golden rule is to ensure the maximum robustness in the way users interact with the system. To give an example, what happens if a server or browser or operating system crashes during or immediately after a credit card transaction has been instigated? Such an unfortunate accident may be unavoidable, but it is incumbent on the e-commerce retailer to send an e-mail to the customer describing the status of the transaction. In turn this requires that e-mail details are gathered before credit card payment is initiated.

It is attention to detail in this regard, seeing the issues from the perspective of the user, that is vital to the establishment of fulfilment mechanisms that work.

So you have taken an order, processed the payment, now you have to deliver. Long before you reach that stage there are many other questions that need answering:

Where can you deliver to?
Where can you take orders from?
What does it cost to deliver?
What does it cost to process an order?
How will you deal with the returns?
How will you forecast the demand?

It is the latter point that will direct your answers to the former. Distribution networks relate to:

Stock control, adequacy of supplies
Warehousing
Stock selection
Packaging
Delivery
Administration.

Discovering where the shortcomings are is complex. There is a famous if perhaps apocryphal story of the wily Internet investor who bought shares in bubble wrap companies. To see a good example of large scale, quality implementation of e-commerce fulfilment it is useful to look at Tesco.com. Questions are raised by the logistics of a large scale e-commerce fulfilment. Should new warehouses be constructed?

Can you Modify your Existing Systems?

At the heart of analysis of these issues lies the forecasting of demand, a notoriously imprecise aspect of the
Internet business. At one end of the scale, if you are a
large concern, and anticipate the Internet will become
the primary channel for distribution, all your operations
will need to be integrated.

This means every component in the supply chain
needs to be aware of an order as soon as it is incurred,
and simultaneously supplies should be prepared in
response to the most accurate possible forecasting.
Systems that perform this function can be purchased
from suppliers such as SAP, Oracle and Invesys. They
have been described as B2B2B2Bob. This bizarre
acronym observes that at each stage of product manu-
facture, order data is passed on instantly, right down to
'Bob', the factory floor worker. The best example of
integration on this scale can be seen at www.dell.com, a
company that owes much of its phenomenal success to
these methods.

Introducing such large integration programs is usually a big project to be attempted only by a big company.
At the other end of the scale entirely is the 'suck it and
see' fulfilment strategy of e-commerce legends such as
eToys.com. It seems unbelievable now, but it is true that
eToys started by taking orders over the web, driving to
Toys 'R' Us and paying cash, driving back to the office,
packaging them and sending them off! This was of
course never intended to be the long-term plan. eToys
were famously proving the principle. Now they have
raised funds, and implemented proper systems. This
approach has merits.

To summarize, if the Internet is obviously going to

be a primary channel for purchase and distribution of your goods and services, develop proper systems and integrate everything and everybody.

If you are not sure of demand, do not invest heavily. Boo.com, the disastrous UK based web sports retailer, provides a classic example of how not to do it. The company launched with over-complicated technology, in more than ten countries simultaneously. The orders were not forthcoming, Boo went bust.

This is not a simple tale of start-ups versus established companies. One of the biggest e-commerce retailers in the UK is Tesco. Yet they still employ people to pick stuff off supermarket shelves manually. That is definitely not the future, but it is how you get to the future.

Consumer Expectations of e-commerce

The formidable reputation of Amazon.com was in part built on their core dedication to deliver quickly. In the UK in 1998 deliveries moved from a few weeks to a few days. This is what people expect. Amazon are famous for managing meteoric growth through rigorous planning.

There is much rubbish spoken about the meaning of brand. In e-commerce, at a practical level, a brand means regular, successful fulfilment of orders, or at least good management of exceptions.

Although many people complain about excessive e-mail, if such communications pertain to a matter of direct interest to the user, they can prove to be a powerful marketing tool. The best e-commerce companies use e-mail to keep their customers informed and connected regarding the status and process of an order, while at all times taking the opportunity to encourage and thank the user. A good pattern of e-mail will take the user through all stages of the buying process:

- Confirmation of order, thank you for choosing XYZ, payment has been taken
- Your order is now in process, we expect delivery will be on X day
- You should by now have received your goods, please call us or e-mail if you are still waiting
- It has been a month since you received your XYZ, we hope it has made you happy. We now have an offer on related items, click here to see . . . etc.

Overall, the logistics of e-commerce delivery are highly complex and variable. It has been said that plans mean nothing but planning is everything. The business benefits of scenario planning are well known and recognized by successful global businesses such as Shell.

We recommend you draw up four or five plans for fulfilment of orders, ranging from small-scale sporadic to very heavy purchases arriving in bursts. If your marketing plan fails, how can you avoid spending too much money on fulfilment systems? If the orders flood in will you be able to marshal the necessary resources of finance, supplies, personnel and administration in reasonable time?

Remember, your reputation is on the line. A brand is built on trust. Great marketing means just one thing: 'DON'T LIE'.

How to Decide if your Business Should Launch a Virtual Presence

There are two answers to this question. The first states that you have no choice, just as a telephone number, postal address, fax and perhaps even e-mail address are the mandatory minimum for any business. From this premise it is axiomatic that a web site is required for every business, whatever it does.

A web site in this analysis is similar to an entry in the vast public telephone book called the Internet. Anyone and everyone will expect you to be in there, so you must be. But the web site can be as simple as a single page with contact details, or as complicated as the human mind can conceive. For example, web sites for leading financial services companies today contain features including:

Access to all services offered by the company
The ability to buy or sell any product offered
Transfer funds in or out
See all products available
Buy or sell shares or other securities
See videos of annual general meetings
See stock prices in real time
Build portfolios online
Calculate any statistical data
Join chat rooms discussing products
Click button to have a sales person telephone you
Choose from a series of languages for your session
Hear music or spoken word
See directories of employees, offices and products
Search the entire web site electronically
See specially commissioned content that is 'scheduled' for 'broadcast'
E-mail questions to the CEO or other investment officers
Read ethical policies, with regard to the environment, socially responsible investment etc.

The above list is still just a small snapshot of what is being delivered today. In the near future we will witness the result of significantly greater investment and attention from thousands of powerful companies around the world. But whatever the investments, all businesses of whatever size face strategic dilemmas around the issue of how and why and when to develop a web presence.

The choices include deciding if a virtual presence should be a simple shop window or primary business channel. This is a very serious issue for every business of stature. The dilemma, or expectation, was brilliantly put by Adam Twiss, co-founder of Zeus Technologies in the *Financial Times* on 11 May 2000. Although only in his early twenties, he understands the big issues exactly when he says, 'From now on it will be the job of every CEO to ensure his (their) company has a robust web server architecture.'

As so often in life, the answer to the question of what to do is dependent on your priorities. For many companies Internet technology can best function simply as a means to schedule appointments, with little perceptible 'value add' from a broader web presence. Such companies can easily go to free sites where booking services can be made for any brand in any colour scheme, such as www.diarymanager.com. Businesses that can benefit from this approach to web-based appointments booking include dentists, lawyers, facilities (e.g. meeting rooms, sports facilities, plumbers, heating experts, electricians, carpenters, tutors and any person who teaches privately, service workers (babysitters, cleaners etc.).

Having described those who perhaps need only a modest web presence, it is useful to look at the other extreme in the scale, a company that depends entirely on the web for its business.

Cisco Systems, one of the five most valuable companies in the world has built itself through acquisition and organic growth, focusing on deploying the technical infrastructure of the Internet.

Cisco's web site at, unsurprisingly, www.cisco.com is one of the world's busiest e-commerce sites, taking several billion dollars of orders each year. What is fascinating about Cisco is the degree to which they have integrated the Internet style of working into their core activities. All time sheets, expenses and central accounting are submitted electronically. It is said that the Cisco finance director has accurate up-to-date management accounts up to the preceding day, every day.

Cisco without doubt represents a shining example of the fully integrated Internet company of the future. In the memorable phrase used by Microsoft programmers working on the development of their NT operating system, as early as possible they would install the prototype software on their own machines and called this process, 'eating your own dog food'. Large companies who are seriously considering using the Internet as a primary channel to acquire and serve users must take this story to heart. It is no solution to find some supplier and spend large sums on large contracts.

To succeed in this environment as a leader you will need to build up material experiential knowledge of the Internet technology and processes internally. To simplify these issues, 'You cannot foist this technology on customers until you are happy with it yourself.'

The days when executive directors of credible companies would leave computing and such like to their secretaries are long gone. Although it is easy to be sympathetic with any individual's frustration with the proprietary character and horrific over-complexity of the Microsoft product suite, nevertheless they are clearly a monopoly supplier, and your customers are forced to suffer stress and anger comparable to yours. Internet browsers, WAP and interactive television are usable in a way Microsoft products never have been. We can look forward to an age when it is possible to use computers without referring to inch-thick manuals.

When those times come, as they must and will, you must decide what resources to apply to your virtual presence.

To summarize the thinking required for this process, ask yourself the following questions:

- Is the Internet going to go away?
- If not, will my competitors use it?
- If they do, will they spend more than us?
- When will the Internet user base stop growing?
- Should I be worried by competitors from abroad?
- Can I compete in other markets and other countries?
- Am I a hunter, or the hunted?
- Do I believe the USA is two years ahead of Europe, or one thousand years behind?

To embellish this final emotive but important point, it is useful to impart two simple but revealing anecdotes regarding Internet pioneers. In the USA WebTV Networks, Inc. was founded in July 1995 with the mission of bringing the Internet into people's living rooms via the television. Some eighteen months later it was acquired by Microsoft for $425 million. WebTV is a classic example of North American leadership in the information technology business. But wait a moment, a sub-$500 Set Top Box showing Internet on TV was demonstrated at London's Café Royal by the British entrepreneur John Bentley in July 1995 after two years of development and before WebTV had even started up. He spent and lost a small fortune, a victim of European indifference to new technology pioneers. Let us hope we can learn the lessons of time.

And here is another lost legend about a young man

called Simon Grice who had been working at CERN in 1991 and went back there in the summer of 1995 and in order to access his e-mail (which was on a server in the UK) he used telnet to hack his way into his ISP's computer. It worked. He read his e-mail – but later realized that very few people would be able to do what he had done and a simpler mechanism was needed. Simon then had an idea for an Internet service that would allow anyone with access to the Internet to access their e-mail by using a browser. Web-based e-mail in other words.

He set about putting a demo together in early 1996 and spent the next year trying to convince people to back the idea. Simon launched the service (www.Pmail.net) and got a few users (under 100,000). At the time UK investors were very unaware of the Internet and could not understand why anyone would want to get their e-mail if not at their own PC !

Hotmail launched an identical service in summer 1996 and was snapped up by Microsoft for $400 million two years later.

CHAPTER 2

Key Issues surrounding e-commerce

There is a single issue that any responsible business must first consider before embarking on an e-commerce strategy, namely, is it sustainable? Most people enjoy the galaxy of international goods that globalization brings to our shores. But the flip side is resource consumption and the harsh realities of global warming. Insurance companies' catastrophic losses caused by climate change are already beginning to de-stabilize world financial systems. Although we all know the climate has changed dramatically in the last thirty years, there is still trite and offensive talk of 'natural cycles'. This folly stands in stark contrast to declarations by informed politicians such as the UK environment minister Michael Meacher who calls climate change 'the greatest challenge in human history'.

We would encourage the reader to analyse this issue in detail, but as a simple first step, if moving to e-commerce will result in any increase in air freight, do not do it. Air travel of people is almost unacceptable. Air travel of goods is unforgivable, for your children's sake, avoid it. In essence, as John Maynard Keynes said, 'It is better to export recipes than cakes'. So, with the ethics speech out of the way, we can look at the technical issues surrounding e-commerce. And do not fear the demise of seaborne transport. Many major firms are already developing big ships based on wind power, hardly a new idea.

Surrounding the enactment of full e-commerce systems are a range of issues embracing access, costs, data protection, fraud and payment security as well as legality and compliance.

These are logistical issues but different in character from conventional planning. Unlike the roads, or ports, or streets, or freight depots of the conventional world, in cyberspace nothing is quite what it seems today, and may become almost anything tomorrow. National legal frameworks are bypassed. Frauds and hackers in any country can attack your systems, and costs incurred to deal with these problems can rise exponentially. Let us deal with these areas in sequence.

Access

In formulation of an e-commerce strategy it is necessary to consider your consumer, or other business audience access to the Internet, as well as your own. At an absolute level, there is not a soul on earth who knows definitively the distribution of browser, PC specifications and access speeds for the world's PC users. And the figures are changing every day.

As part of your e-commerce planning you will need to consider both the size of your possible existing market and growth trends. This thinking needs to be correlated to a minimum machine specification. From this cross matching you will be able to project potential market size.

To present a methodology for planning, start by obtaining figures for PC presentation and use in your market. Research agencies such as Forrester, IDC and

Nielsen can provide this for a fee. Or try searching the archives of free newspaper web sites, such as FT.com.

If we look at some imaginary figures that bear no correlation to reality, they can reveal how you can make decisions regarding investment and market reach.

INVENTED RESEARCH	2000	2001	2002
PC users number in the UK	15m	20m	25m
With Internet access	10m	15m	20m
Processor			
Pentium or better	7m	14m	20m
486 or worse	3m	1m	0m
Browser			
Netscape or Microsoft 5.0 or better	2m	8m	17m
Netscape or Microsoft 4.0 or better	6m	7m	3m
Netscape or Microsoft 3.0 or worse	2m	0m	0m
Interactive TV users	1m	5m	10m
WAP users	1m	4m	12m
UK Internet access as a percentage of world market	10%	8%	6%

The imaginary figures in the table would allow the e-commerce planner to come to some simple conclusions. Firstly, that it is probably OK to deliver to browsers of

4.0 and above, but not 5.0, until around 2002. Also that WAP and interactive TV are relatively unimportant channels this year, but will become vital next year. And that means you have to plan for their deployment now. What network providers are there, what is the deal?

To look at the main access factors individually for the PC:

Processor. PCs contain sometimes hundreds of micro-chips but one chip controls all the others and this is referred to as the CPU, central processing unit or commonly, the 'processor'. Because all parts of the PC depend upon this central brain it is the key component. The market is completely dominated by Intel and it is the Intel product range that defines the levels of power. A simple division is between the 486 range of processors and earlier, which can support a simple web browser but little else simultaneously, and the Pentium range that has more significant capability.

Browser. An Internet browser is a software application that can, when launched, search for Internet connectivity, initiate it if it is not present, then automatically serve to view the default screen. From this point onwards, so long as it does not crash, and web connectivity is maintained, it is possible to use the browser to view any site on the Internet.

There are however some serious issues that influence browser performance and capability. The two main site developments to challenge older browsers are 'frames' and 'Java'. Frames are a simple mechanism for reducing the time required to download pages. Frames can also provide a significant aid to navigation. All browsers of 4.0 and above support frames. Java is the name of a coffee. The computer language Java was written by developers at Sun Microsystems who stayed up very late at night and drank a lot of coffee, hence the name. Behind Java is a simple idea. If a browser is Java enabled, it can operate as a Java Virtual Machine. This allows, in effect, for the browser to become a miniature software driven computer. Because the functionality sits in the browser, web sites attain the ability to make dynamic calculations independent of any particular PC architecture. All browsers of 4.0 and above support Java. However, great care needs to be exercised before introducing Java functionality into a web site. Specifically, it can make sites very slow, and often unstable.

Other technologies have developed that further challenge browsers. A good example is Flash, a popular system for presenting text and graphics in a more animated format. These can challenge older browsers, thereby frustrating users. A more profound technology shift is the move to embrace streamed media such as audio and video. The heavy demands of these technologies challenge even the best processors, with the newest browsers and fastest connections.

Speed of Connection. This is a fundamental access issue. It is often said that the world is dividing into information haves and have nots. But even inside the connected community there is a stark divide between people who have broadband, or at least high speed access, typically corporate users, on corporate networks, and the home user struggling with a modem on a normal phone line. To start with the home user, communication bandwidth has been delivered to the home until now through a technology enchantingly described as POTS or Plain Old Telephone Service. When you speak into your telephone, a membrane vibrates generating a modulation of electrical disturbance described as analogue because it is analogous to a voice pattern.

All Internet access devices operate using digital technology. It is therefor necessary for a modem to both 'modulate' and then 'de-modulate' digital data to communicate and this process is laborious.

At the other extreme is the corporate Internet user. Typically medium and large companies will establish relations with a supplier of broadband Internet connectivity, usually as part of a bulk telecommunications contract. In fact the day will soon arrive when telephone connectivity is simply a sub-set of Internet.

As a result of bulk business-to-business connectivity purchase, corporate users tend to enjoy very high speed Internet access. So as a general rule, if you are in the B2B market-place you can be more ambitious regarding the technology you deploy.

Golden Rule. To summarize the access issue, if you aspire to trade with large numbers of consumers, you need to establish a robust, simple, popular system specification. Employ the KISS principle at all times: Keep It Simple, Stupid!

As an effective means to check you are staying true to the needs of your audience, follow this simple process:

1. Buy an old, second hand early Pentium or 486.
2. Load it with an older browser, 4.0 etc.
3. Connect it with a 28.8K modem over a POTS line.
4. Use this machine for evaluation of any e-commerce development you propose to sign off and implement.

If you stick to the above four-step plan, you will not go wrong. We are sorry to quote them so often, but this was another error made by Boo.com.

It is always instructive to look at the industry leader, Yahoo.com. A cursory look at the Yahoo! web site will show that it is very simple to look at, it hardly ever changes, and uses text over graphics most of the time. It is no coincidence that it is the most popular web site on earth.

Internet professionals have such respect for Yahoo! that they have developed an industry standard measurement for the speed of a web site called 'Speed to Yahoo!'. What this means is that to measure how well your web site performs you should literally time it with a stop watch against Yahoo!. Speed of response from a web site is probably the primary determinant of it's likely popularity and success. Remember www: the World Won't Wait.

Understanding the extreme detail of what makes a web site fast or slow is quite complex. It is in part dependent on the overall network load, with peaks in North American Internet use typically having a negative influence on response times. However, as a simple ready reckoner you can consider the following approximate split:

One third server code. The more elegantly your software is written, the faster it will operate.

One third server speed. Do you have thousands of powerful mini computers, or are you trying to serve a thousand users on a 486?

One third bandwidth. Is your e-commerce strategy dependent on a home highway line from BT or is it professionally hosted at a major ISP?

Accelerating web site speed will for many years continue to be a key issue for business. Leading companies such as Yahoo! have been developing highly sophisticated systems such as 'predictive caching' that analyse your last web interaction to guess what is likely to be next, thereby freeing processor power.

Other factors that can influence speed of download include a possible requirement to obtain advertising from ad-servers that may be slow to respond. This can form an argument for larger players to sell their own advertising. Web statistic companies can also provide a retardant to performance.

Throughout all this process, remember the golden rule and test it all on a low specification machine. That is what many of your customers will experience. Make sure you do too.

Costs

When approaching costing for e-commerce it is tempting to ask how long is a piece of string. There are more rational ways to answer the question. Basic principles to consider include:

- To what degree are you prepared to outsource and partner?
- To what degree are you experimenting?
- What are the milestones that will trigger stages of investment?
- How much in-house expertise do you have?
- How much resource can you afford to use to maintain the site?
- What economies of scale do you envisage?

As a general rule of thumb, it is less expensive to buy equipment and hire resources in-house. But such assets as you may acquire will have to be depreciated, and may become liabilities if they are badly specified or inadequate.

Typical stages of e-commerce development can be summarized as follows:

Start-up/small scale operation

Limited equipment will be purchased in-house, on a small-scale connection, or may be hosted with the web design agency. Payment gateways subcontracted to third parties such as Worldpay and Verisign. Typical annual cost: £10,000 to £150,000. User base that might be served: 1,000 to 50,000 user sessions per month.

Medium-sized operation

Own equipment or leased equipment hosted inside industry facility. Payment gateway options increase, dependant on brand recognition and trust.

Typical annual cost: £150,000 to £2m. User base that might be served: 50,000 to 500,000 user sessions per month.

Large-scale operation

Entire ownership of equipment, staffing etc., combined with supplier service support guarantees. Payment gateway fully integrated into internal treasury operation. Typical annual cost: £2m to £80m. User base that might be served: 500,000 to multimillion user sessions per month.

Data protection

An individual or organization using the Internet to exchange information with members of the public or other companies carries certain responsibilities defined under the UK Data Protection Act 1998. We strongly recommend that you study this in full. It can be found at http://www.legislation.hmso.gov.uk/acts/acts1998/199 80029.htm

It will be useful to give here the key components.

'Data' means information which

(a) is being processed by means of equipment operating automatically in response to instructions given for that purpose,

(b) is recorded with the intention that it should be processed by means of such equipment,

(c) is recorded as part of a relevant filing system or with the intention that it should form part of a relevant filing system,

(d) does not fall within paragraph (a) (b) or (c) but forms part of an accessible record as defined by section 68: (i) a health record as defined by subsection (2), (ii) an educational record as defined by Schedule 11, or (iii) an accessible public record as defined by Schedule 12.

'Sensitive personal data' means personal data consisting of information as to

(a) the racial or ethnic origin of the data subject,

(b) his political opinions,

(c) his religious beliefs or other beliefs of a similar nature,

(d) whether he is a member of a trade union (within the meaning of the Trade Union and Labour Relations (Consolidation) Act 1992),

(e) his physical or mental health or condition,

(f) his sexual life,

(g) the commission or alleged commission by him of any offence, or

(h) any proceedings for any offence committed or alleged to have been committed by him, the disposal of such proceedings or the sentence of any court in such proceedings.

Subject to the following provisions of this section and to sections 8 and 9, an individual is entitled

(a) to be informed by any data controller whether

personal data of which that individual is the data subject are being processed by or on behalf of that data controller,

(b) if that is the case, to be given by the data controller a description of (i) the personal data of which that individual is the data subject, (ii) the purposes for which they are being or are to be processed, and (iii) the recipients or classes of recipients to whom they are or may be disclosed,

(c) to have communicated to him in an intelligible form (i) the information constituting any personal data of which that individual is the data subject, and (ii) any information available to the data controller as to the source of those data.

An individual who suffers damage by reason of any contravention by a data controller of any of the requirements of this Act is entitled to compensation from the data controller for that damage.

So you have been warned! Also note that you need to register with the Commissioner responsible for data protection:

Subject to the following provisions of this section, personal data must not be processed unless an entry in respect of the data controller is included in the register maintained by the Commissioner under section 19 (or is treated by notification regulations made by virtue of section 19(3) as being so included).

A notification under this section must specify in accordance with notification regulations (a) the registrable particulars, and (b) a general description of measures to be taken for the purpose of complying with the seventh data protection principle.

A person must not knowingly or recklessly, without

the consent of the data controller (a) obtain or disclose personal data or the information contained in personal data, or (b) procure the disclosure to another person of the information contained in personal data. *(Crown copyright 1998, with the permission of the Controller of Her Majesty's Stationery Office.)*

Fraud and Payment Security

The Internet is a wonderful thing, but there are dangers. Trust is the key. There are companies you will trust, and companies you won't, and the one thing that makes us decide is branding. However, the Internet is essentially unregulated, so URLs are key guarantors of bona fide identity.

IBM.com, Tesco.com, Amazon.com we have heard of, we trust them. But what about 'www.quickpay.nl.' Will you give them your credit card details, even if they display a familiar logo? If you type them into a web site the transaction can theoretically be processed at any value, in any country. If there were to be a problem, who would you call, in what country, under what jurisdiction or law? The United Nations is beginning to help develop a framework of international law in this area but it is early days. In the meantime there are many stories of people being swindled, typically by sites offering pornography, where excessive charges are made against credit cards and the culprits cannot easily be identified.

There is significant public concern that card details are intercepted in transit by hackers, but this is seldom if ever the case. Most card frauds are the result of details being stolen from bona fide commercial organizations, either electronically or in person, or through the generation of random credit card numbers by thieves who hit upon your number by chance. Either way, the risk is not dissimilar to conventional use of the card.

This is a material problem. As the *Financial Times* reported on 7 June 2000: 'Credit and debit card crime on the internet amounts to between 1 and 2 per cent of total transactions and the problem is "definitely rising", says the credit card research group, APACS. Meanwhile, figures from credit card companies suggest this kind of fraud has doubled since 1998. The surge of internet crime comes at a time when the world is on the brink of an explosion in e-commerce. By 2004, online spending in business-to-consumer markets will grow to Euro 417bn from Euro 44bn this year.'

Trusted third parties are beginning to emerge such as VeriSign and Worldpay, but these new brands will take a long time to win consumer trust. There are various other solutions to the problem in train. Some of the most exciting technological developments relate to purchase of goods and services using payment authorized and transacted via mobile phone providers.

There are many dramatic predictions for potential future use of mobile telephones including integrated payment gateways. They range from buying tickets for travel or the theatre, to share trading, shopping and downloading media assets such as music files. Researchers at IDC predict that by 2002 there will be more wireless subscribers with Internet access than wired subscribers. Gartner Group also predict that by 2004 an astonishing 40 per cent of all business-to-consumer transactions will be conducted through mobile devices.

Other solutions include ever more sophisticated encryption of communications, from so-called 128 bit to 512 or more. But these security measures do not always effectively address the underlying cause of problems, and heavy encryption technologies can often fall foul of national security legislation.

Interactive television will change the world completely. This is a bold statement but it is based on firm foundations. There have already been two revolutions in the way the industrialized world relates to itself. Firstly radio, then television. Interactive television will break the hegemony and in two or three years will experience exactly the same payment and security problems as the Internet accessed on PC. But short term, the dominant UK providers such as Open . . . are constructing so called 'walled gardens' where approved retailers are offered to consumers in a controlled environment. The obvious advantage of this system is that it provides immediate validation to users of the authenticity of vendors. But the jury is out regarding providers' ability to turn high security into juicy profits in the interactive television, walled garden model.

Security

In this area rank amateurism pervades the operations of too many companies. Just as keeping the server operational has become an overwhelming imperative, an effective security policy is also a basic requirement. However, the general picture is bleak. A recent DTI report explains that 62 per cent of UK organizations have experienced some form of security breach, and less than a fifth have a formal information management security policy in place.

The now infamous 'Love bug' did enormous damage to businesses across the world, although experts report it could have been far worse. The focus on Jpeg and MP3 files left most business applications unharmed. But what if spreadsheets and word files had been destroyed? About 85 per cent of the cost of office equipment goes into computers and software. It is worth carefully considering their vulnerabilities, and how to avoid disaster.

At the very least, make sure all your staff know not to open any e-mail attachments from unknown sources.

Business detests uncertainty, so the natural response to managing the risks of internet security failure would logically be to take out an insurance policy. Unfortunately there is very little available at present in the UK. A Lloyds of London company called Hiscox Insurance offers a product called Cyberliability that was launched in 1999. It covers breaches of rights, including issues such as e-mail that is defamatory or disclosure of confidential information, as well as cyber-vandalism or hacking and fraud, with liability protection of up to £10 million. Such a policy would not cover damage caused by anything like the 'I love you' virus.

The high level issues for management are well explained by Gil Shwed, CEO of Check Point Software Technologies, quoted in the *Financial Times* on 7 June 2000: 'Today, if you manage security for a company, you are in charge of defining users and defining policies. Now how do you control the same environment when you have to give network access to perhaps thousands of companies in which you do not know who the users are?'

Dr Neil Barrett, technical director of Information Risk Management in London, was quoted as feeling jaundiced about e-commerce: 'I have taken out so many hackers' systems and seen so many credit card numbers on their computers – including my own credit card number – that I barely use the internet for e-commerce.' In essence, the overriding principles are clear. It is hard to imagine anybody entering into e-commerce relationships except with someone they would in any case trust on the high street. Furthermore, all right thinking people should check their credit and debit card statements with great care.

Legality and compliance

The speed of the e-commerce revolution has caught companies and legislators alike unprepared. The compliance department of a bank would typically ensure that any written communication 'complied' with applicable legislation. How can that process be implemented in new media. when a web site may change hourly, or by the second? Some rudimentary international standards are emerging.

The ICC or International Chamber of Commerce is a global business organization with significant membership including ABB, AT&T, BT, Cadbury Schweppes, Citicorp, Coca-Cola, Exxon, Ford, HSBC, IBM, KPMG, Mitsubishi, NEC, P&G, Shell, Sony, Toyota and Unilever. They offer summary advice regarding liability and compliance that can be seen at www.iccwbo.org.

In the view of the ICC the use of model contracts provides a flexible, market-based solution for meeting differing data protection standards in the conduct of global business. Business strongly supports the use of partnership working groups between business and government – such as the OECD Technical Advisory Groups – to address the numerous taxation issues relating to electronic commerce. Business is working with tax authorities to open this process broadly to interested business participants.

The ICC offers a range of Model Clauses that e-commerce companies can incorporate into their contracts by inserting the following sentence, or a similar one, into their written agreements:

'The parties hereto agree that the ICC Model Clauses For Use In Contracts Involving Transborder Data Flows, Publication No.____ (1998), are hereby incorporated by reference in this agreement as if fully set out herein.'

At the ICC web site detailed definitions are given applying to the terminology used in contracts. The Model Clauses cover a variety of useful areas including:

Warranties of the Data Exporter
Undertakings of the Data Exporter and Disputes with Data Subjects or Data Protection Authorities
Warranties of the Data Importer
Undertakings of the Data Importer
Dispute Resolution
Indemnities
Termination
Data Processors
Governing Law

Key issues surrounding e-commerce
If you want to open a shop, build a factory or expand overseas, there are many examples of good practice to follow: employ builders or agents, set budgets and timetables, ensure your project finance is adequate, etc. In this new world of e-commerce, however, a checklist of the main issues that need to be addressed may be useful.

- Is your proposed service environmentally acceptable? Does it depend on air freight?
- What research can you obtain regarding internet users, and the equipment specification?
- What decisions can you make regarding investment based on these figures?
- What is the minimum specification machine you will direct your service at?

- What browser and speed of connection will you assume as lowest acceptable?
- How fast does the site need to be and how can you check it on your minimum specification machine?
- What budget are you allocating for delivering the site?
- What budget are you allocating for the daily management and development of the site?
- Are you registered with the data protection registrar?
- What policies do you have in place to minimize the risks of security breaches?
- How are you defended against hackers?
- How are you ensuring compliance with the law in each country?
- How are you assessing possible liability, and can this risk be insured?

CHAPTER 3

Moving your Business to the Web

ANALYSING YOUR BUSINESS

The year 2000 has seen some startling reversals of fortune. In February and March the craze for technology stocks was at its peak. Attention directed at the new economy was so great it was eclipsing the behemoths of the traditional, or so called 'old' economy. Unilever for example, saw its share price halve over twelve months for no other reason than an obsession with new media amongst investors. This was reversed with the technology stock fall in April and May. Some sanity or equilibrium is returning.

Furthermore, these fluctuations have been completely indiscriminate. To look at Unilever again, it is indeed perverse to punish the company because of Internet developments. Value is often created in e-commerce through the removal of an expensive layer of administration between manufacturer and consumer. This process, called disintermediation, lies at the heart of e-commerce economics. And of course nobody can disintermediate Unilever. So let us come to an understanding of how the e-commerce market is developing by looking at the first victims of the revolution, and extrapolating to the more secure sectors.

Immediate potential losers from e-commerce

Insurance brokers
Travel agents
Record and book shops
Paper based directories and listings
Computer hardware and software retailers
Car sellers
Estate agents
Letter post services
Classified newspaper advertisers
Recruitment consultants
Private client stockbrokers

Medium-term losers from e-commerce

Banks, insurance companies, investment managers
Telecommunication companies dependant on voice traffic
Television companies without Internet migration plans
Specialist goods retailers
All intermediaries such as wholesalers, agents, and market makers
Aspects of department stores
Book and magazine publishers without Internet strategies
Commercial property companies with outdated assets
Car companies (their p.e. ratios are already very low)
Educational institutions. Learning is often better delivered online

Safer sectors, fairly immune to e-commerce threat

> Location-based services, e.g. hotels, theatres, cinemas
> Consumer goods manufacturers such as Unilever
> Data-enabled communication companies, e.g. COLT, MCI Worldcom, Level3, Qwest etc.
> Computer companies, e.g. Dell, HP, Compaq etc.
> Infrastructure providers, e.g. Cisco, Marconi, Global crossing.
> Mobile device suppliers such as Nokia, Ericsson and Motorola
> Video communications companies such as Sony, Eye-Network.com and Polyspan
> Interactive television companies such as NTL, Open . . . and Liberate
> Application service providers, offering software over networks such as Cable & Wireless plc and EDS
> Delivery services such as UPS and TNT
> Food providers like McDonalds and Burger King

If your company is in either of the first two categories, you need to make e-commerce happen quickly. If you are in the third category, you are either safe from the impact of revolution, or are in a sector making it happen.

In essence the issue is simple: do you produce goods or services that a competitor can offer more efficiently online? If so, act now. You face a crisis. In Chinese the ideograph for the word crisis is a combination of two words 'threat' and 'opportunity'.

Problems and advantages of moving to the web
Adopting a global mindset can be seen as a key challenge for national businesses. A major UK bank can for

example find it difficult to grasp that a US competitor may arrive to cherrypick their customers.

If a web site crashes from unanticipated numbers of visitors, that is a problem. But if a fully operational e-commerce site fails, that is an aberration. Given the bonanza of speculative investment created by the e-commerce tidal wave, it can be very difficult to attract and keep competent employees. The best people demand and usually receive equity or stock options. Yet these demands often force quoted companies to demerge their Internet operations as a separate entity.

The heart of the problem for a large company considering migration to an e-commerce platform is the potential risk of service failure. In the conventional media environment, a single customer service representative may be a bit rude, or a piece of paper may be lost, but overall the system is a sum of its parts, and trust is built through the aggregation of numerous transactions. On the Internet, for any one territory or language, all your eggs are well and truly in one basket.

As in so many of the issues we have seen concerning e-commerce, what makes the glass half empty is the same thing that makes it half full. Because a single country or language can all be processed through a single web site URL it becomes possible to scale up your operation at phenomenal speed. A single company such as Charles Schwab can come to dominate the buying and selling of shares in the USA, from a standing start, in a couple of years, from a single URL, using servers in a single principal location, at minuscule marginal cost per additional user. Try doing that with manual execution of orders!

In the old days a firm aspiring to compete on such a scale would be obliged to hire large numbers of employees, and provide them with premises, train them and motivate them. Large computers, performing billions of calculations per second, never need to halt. No coffee breaks, no family distractions, no trips to the loo. In the old economy, the only way to compete was to try and squeeze even greater marginal efficiency out of employees. This was always hard, often fruitless work that honoured neither party well.

Creating a new web site
In the mid 1990s when we first started to advise corporations regarding development of their web presence, it became clear there was distance between the technology people and the marketing department. It has been a slow process but this divide is slowly being bridged. Now that the Internet has evolved into a mainstream, perhaps central, issue for business, new standards are emerging. 'Web site' is perhaps something of a misnomer. We should instead refer to your 'web process'. A web site should not and cannot be a brochure. It may be best to consider your web presence as a new division managed by a team that may include representations from:

Sales (the big issue in all commerce)
Marketing (getting people to the site)
Editorial (creating and editing content)
IT (making sure the site works)
Operations (planning to service demand)
Finance (budgets and evaluation of Return on Investment)
Warehouse (the logistical challenges of fulfilment)
Personnel (do you want to hire staff?)
Investor relations (information for shareholders)
PR (positive messages out, and defence against accusations)
Procurement (do you want to offer contracts?)

Community affairs (tell of your company giving something back)
Environment management (this is about your reputation)
Chief Executive (statement by the boss/leader)

The process for developing the basic architecture and roll-out of a web site is fairly simple. The real art comes in the area of identifying functionality and attracting traffic. To deal with the simple stages:

1. Identify the purpose of the web site. In a sense its 'mission statement'. To quote the three-stage plan developed by the Design Council; focus on the outcome, focus on the outcome and focus on the outcome.
2. Establish the measures required to manage the site each year.
3. Establish the resources required to manage the site each year.
4. Define the marketing plan for the site. How can you make people visit it? This includes obvious steps such as putting your URL on every communication, through to TV and poster advertising.
5. Appoint the team.
6. Appoint the consultants and suppliers.
7. Establish the timetable, finalize the budget.

Larger web sites now often include a user interface evaluation stage or stages through the development process. Where development budgets are in the millions, just as with large scale advertising expenditure, consumer focus groups can offer a comfort factor.

Working effectively with agencies
Technology is a peculiar and perhaps challenging media

for project managers. In our experience it can be the person who says 'no' that saves the day. A major oil company launched a very successful internal CD-ROM guide in 1994 with a range of features including a database of petrol station layouts, videos, diagrams, word and excel files and complex animations. All of this was delivered on time and within budget, in part because the project manager at the client side refused to entertain any bright ideas hatched on the way to completion. Conversely, we also witnessed a major US financial services company fail to deliver their European web presence in any form of orderly fashion because every possible feature was accepted, and thereby effectively none were delivered. This process whereby projects slip into anarchy is called 'project creep'; avoid it.

Briefing designers
People tend not to tell their surgeons where to make incisions, or suggest to chefs how to cook. But everyone has a designer in them bursting to get out. Our advice is simple; avoid trying to tell designers how to do their jobs. Choose the right partners in terms of IT, design and integration, and from that point try to monitor but not interfere. Accept that within their area of competence they know better than you.

URLs
A Universal Resource Locator (URL) is a web site address, or domain name. It can form an important part of your web strategy. The Internet is a most peculiar and surprising new entity, respecting no location. One lyric web analyst observed that registering a new URL is like a sperm impregnating an egg, the beginning of a great new potential. At a more direct level, your URL is how people are going to find you. Web URLs such as

sports.com, oil.com, money.com etc. now change hands for millions of dollars.

Rebranding an existing web site

Branding is a complicated word, or is it? It is certainly true that more and more people are spending more and more time talking about branding. In essence there are two definitions of the word. The complex one states that a brand is every aspect of a customer's interaction with your organization, from the behaviour of a receptionist to the livery of a lorry. Maybe brand even means the soul of your organization.

There is a much simpler definition that we can use here. Your brand is the way your organization presents itself in terms of the company logo, colours, typefaces and general design and photographic style. In particular branding is about the consistency in the use of the above elements. The mind builds up a sense of brand in large measure from consistent exposure to consistently presented visual clues.

As *Design Week* magazine observed in November 1997, 'The explosion of Internet use is forcing multinational companies to step up global branding and creating an increase in high-profile identity projects. Multinationals are looking to standardise identities because the range of local brands and marques appearing on international websites is giving users mixed messages. With marketing departments increasingly taking over website management from IT departments the issue is being treated particularly seriously. Unilever's marketing department is aware of the dangers of "brand schizophrenia". "In a globalising world we recognise the need to manage identity to prevent it becoming too fragmented. However, we also recognise the need to retain a local element," says Unilever new media manager Maggie Huddy.'

Our experience backs this up. We are asked again and again by clients wanting to create a coherent identity both for the companies in their portfolio and their branches across the world. Achieving a consistent identity is key. It allows you to look coherent and co-ordinated, not fragmented and confused.

Rebranding your existing web site should be an exercise intended to ensure each part of your organization reflects the corporate whole. Each page does not have to look exactly the same, but they need to be seen to emanate from the same central core. Having said that, is it wrong to have a completely consistent grid and navigation across your entire site? Probably not.

Keeping things simple, what to keep in, what to cut
Good web site development starts with a clear sense of what you want to achieve. From this point you can move on to very careful review of content and structure. What content is required to achieve your stated goals? Do not think what you have got; think instead about what you need.

In collaboration with your web team consider the structure of the site, the home page and next level of navigation. What are the key questions or divisions that lead to a content structure? For BT.com our early work revealed the obvious question: 'Is this for your home or business?'. For BT there were substantially different product ranges and styles of communication suited to each audience. The web site needed to address these as early as possible.

Next consider the user's journey around the site. It can be tempting to structure a web site so it imitates or replicates the structure of your business, but is that sensible? What does the user need to know, and how are they going to find that information. A consistent navigational system is a very good idea. Buttons should stay as consistent as possible from page to page. Make sure that you always have a link back to the homepage on every page, perhaps through a text link or a link from the company logo. This gives a way out if the user is stuck. We also strongly recommend you include a search function.

As a golden rule, remember that computers can do incredible things. But a PC screen makes a poor brochure. Moving your literature to the web is to miss the point, and that activity goes by the slanderous name of 'brochureware'.

Make sure your site can actually do things for users. E-commerce is about fulfilment. Give real-time prices, live quotes, giant databases of information, links to other sites. The Internet is an exciting place to put on a show. Forget the old corporate speak and gobbledegook.

Avoiding cobwebs – the challenge of site maintenance
At heart there are a number of simple principles:

A web site is for life, not just for Christmas.
It is much more a new process or channel that your business adopts, rather than a project with a definite end point.
A web site is the beginning, like launching a new logo. On the day it is released, the work starts in earnest.
You can spend £100 million on the best technology there is but that is still no reason to believe anyone will visit your web site.
It does not matter how good the technology is if it looks bad.
If the site does nothing useful it will make your company look aimless.

CHAPTER 4

Customer relationships – your virtual tone of voice

The Internet is changing language. It is inevitable that it should do so. The change is perhaps not so great as to warrant clichés of the 'It will never be the same again' variety. Language will still be a recognizable sister of its former self, many of the traditional elements of effective communication will remain just as important as ever. But things are – and will be – different. In this chapter we'll look at:

> The role of language in e-commerce – the role has changed and will probably continue to change
> What makes effective e-commerce language – short, sharp, packed with personality
> Some things to avoid – the dead hand, the windy, the wild.

Two types of change

One thing we can be sure of is that the Internet is affecting language in two distinct ways: it is changing the importance of language, and it is changing the way we use language.

These two elements have quite different explanations, and we'll deal with each in turn.

Why is language so centrally important on the Net? The answer lies in the difference between the ways in which virtual and non-virtual companies interact with their customers.

Consider, for a moment, an old-style bricks and mortar company. Through what channels does it interact with its customers? What, in other words, are the building blocks of its identity? Four things come to mind: its products, its physical outlets, its employees, its marketing material.

These four elements are probably of roughly equal importance. Together they constitute the brand and the promise this brings for customers. The balance of importance of each of these elements depends, of course, on the type of company we're talking about; some will rely more on advertising campaigns to make an impact, some on customer service. But it is fair to say that the all four components will all play a significant part in determining the identity of any bricks and mortar company you could care to mention.

Another notable feature is the limited importance of the written word in the four factors mentioned above. In fact, the written word has almost nothing to do with a company's products or its physical outlets, only a partial contribution to make to its customer relations in terms of responding to customer letters and e-mails – indeed actions are often as important as words and a significant but by no means dominant role in its marketing material.

Now let's turn to the identity of a virtual business. Virtual businesses also have products, physical existences, employees and marketing. But do these things all bear to the same extent on a company's identity?

The answer is a definite no. The role of products is unchanged; after all, products are something that every company must have. But what about physical outlets? Virtual businesses have offices and warehouses – which the customers will never see – and in most cases nothing else. No shops, no branches. No bricks-and-mortar existence at all.

What about employees? Those of a virtual business will certainly interact with customers, but not on a live, face-to-face basis. Only, in fact, through written communications, in most cases e-mails.

And finally, what about marketing? Well marketing does happen, but often not through the traditional route of direct mail. For a virtual company has a fifth, novel way of interacting with its customers – its web site. And this web site is not just another component of corporate identity, with little bearing on any of the others. To the customer the web site – its functionality, look, content and style – *is* the business. In fact, its overall impact is to seriously negate many of the others.

And on any web site the language takes centre stage. Get it stodgy or brusque and customers click away elsewhere. Make it full of hype and boastfulness and they try elsewhere again.

The Internet and language

Why is the Internet changing language? This question is harder to answer than you might initially think. One of the problems is that, while everyone has an opinion as to how significant the Internet is, no one has a very clear notion of precisely why this is the case.

Of course, certain words and concepts come easily to mind: speed, accessibility, interactivity. But what do these words really mean, in practical terms? And how do they relate to specifics like the way a business communicates with its customers?

Let us start with speed. The Internet, as everyone

knows, is a fast medium. Information travels from one place to another in a fraction of a second. No more waiting around for letters to be delivered. No more struggling with reams of fax roll. It also speeds things up by making us move less. It significantly reduces the need to travel. Want a book? Instead of going to a library or bookshop, go to Amazon.com. Want groceries? Just go to your online for your supermarket of choice. Want to book a hotel room? Online can help there too.

It's not only that you don't need to travel. Activities themselves become less drawn out, less cumbersome. All the delays that used to be a part of everyday life – queues in shops, waits for assistants – no longer affect us. Microchips, unlike people, can do more than one thing at once.

As a result of all this, our expectations also change. We no longer expect to dawdle over things. When we're browsing the web, we want things to happen fast. We're more likely to know what we want, and be impatient of not getting it. Browsing and window-shopping, in fact, may become things of the past. In the future, it might be a choice between buy quick or buy nothing.

What does all this mean for language and writing? How will communication differ as a result of this speeded up, more exacting environment?

In the first place, writing will get briefer. By this, we don't mean that there will be fewer words in total. But each individual piece of writing will have to be shorter and more incisive. To put it bluntly, people will have less time to linger over what they read. So writing will have to become less bulky. The rule with web sites is that people need to access information as speedily as possible and with as little fuss as possible. The figures seem to indicate that over 50 per cent of online buys are never completed because people simply get bored with going through the process of basket filling and form completion online.

Writing will also need to be more relevant. Just as people won't have time to wade through reams of verbiage, so they'll be less patient of waffle and fluff. They'll want to get to the information quickly, not linger over laborious introductions and meandering anecdotes. So focused writing will come into its own.

Writing will need to be clearer, too. If people are in a hurry, they don't want to get tripped up by opaque phrases whose meaning doesn't jump instantly off the page; they'll be more likely to click off and go elsewhere. Great pains have to be taken over making every word as plain and as intelligible as possible.

So here are the rules: keep the language relevant, don't waffle, distil everything down to its essence without losing all personality, and make it easy but not patronizing.

Easy access

The Internet dramatically increases the potential reach of the written word. Set up a newspaper in Outer Mongolia, and it will be read by a few hundred people at most. Set up a web site, and it will be accessible to the whole world.

There's only one limitation – language. Very few people speak Mongolian, so the chances are that a Mongolian web site won't have the rest of the world logging on. But let's change the scenario. Set up a site in London. Now how many people will be able to understand it? Only the entire English-speaking world, and all those from other nations who speak English as a second language. It's impossible to know the exact figure, but we're talking more than a billion.

That is mind-blowing potential. And it has important implications for the way we use language. We'll need to write in a way that excludes as few of those billion or so potential customers as possible. So writing will need to be simple, clear and cosmopolitan. We'll need to avoid exclusive in-jokes or references, jargon and complex phrasings or words. It's no good being locally-preoccupied.

Will language become less colourful as a result? Perhaps. After all, local touches often add flavour to writing. But this only means that businesses will have to find new ways of grabbing large and diverse audiences in ways which don't exclude certain groups from the picture.

At the same time, it is worth remembering that a more cosmopolitan web site language will co-exist with the more tailored possibilities of Internet marketing. In some cases, businesses will have to use language which is universally accessible. In others, they'll be able to communicate in a far more focused, targeted way, perhaps reaching individuals in exactly their own voice and style.

So be inclusive with the language, avoid in-jokes or national-specific styles, be cosmopolitan and fresh.

E-commerce utilizes the web to promote, display and sell products. And the web, unlike traditional media, is interactive.

Customers who choose to visit a web site can also choose to leave. While there, the customer controls what he or she wants to see. It is the customer who clicks on some icons as opposed to others, who issues orders to view these pages, not those. In terms of language, this means that businesses will have to adopt a less dictatorial tone. On the web, you can't bully the customer in the same way as you could in an old brochure or instruction leaflet. Instead, your tone will have to be helpful and suggestive, more focused and polite.

It is important to make the most of the interactive nature of the web. After all it is the globe's greatest-ever conversation. So encourage feedback. Accept customer power. One way of judging the success of your language is to look at how many people bother to interact with your site via e-mail. If you get lots of hits but few follow up e-mails then the chances are your site is boring people rigid.

So the rules are: embrace interactivity, don't be dictatorial, be adult-to-adult.

The single, connecting theme to all the changes detailed above is that the power and status of the customer has been and will continue to be greatly enhanced by the Internet. The power relationship between business and consumer has been tilted in favour of the latter.

This is probably a good thing for everyone. For the consumer, the advantages are obvious. More choice, better service, more accountability, more responsiveness. People will no longer feel chained to certain services which no longer satisfy them simply because of a lack of alternatives.

For business, too, this erosion of power is probably a good thing, because lack of consumer choice before the arrival of the Internet did not equate to a better deal for all businesses. Rather, it meant a better deal for a few – generally large – organizations who were, over time, able to drive out small-scale competitors and literally colonize the physical market-place.

By contrast, the Internet's lower overheads and the lack of any physical barriers to competition mean that smaller companies are much better placed to make a real go of offering their own, more specialized products and services to a wide range of people. Small companies in the past lacked reach, which could only be obtained by building expensive physical outlets across a large area and by high-budget marketing campaigns, both of which were beyond their means. On the Internet, each company has a similar potential reach, no matter how large or small it is. For a start, advertising can be more targeted and less expensive and, even more crucially, the Internet's inherent interactivity allows customers to go out searching for services in a way they were never able to do previously.

The result is that, if you have something which people will genuinely want, you are more likely to succeed in making a go of turning it into a business. And a world where genuine demand is satisfied, as opposed to the high-profile marketing of products which people do not always necessarily want, can only be a good thing, for customers and businesses alike.

Talking to the newly empowered customer

How should the empowered customer be addressed? What tone of voice should you adopt? How should your communications reflect the more equal power relationship?

Partly, it's a matter of following all the old rules of good writing. A non-captive audience will be less tolerant of sloppiness, obscurity or condescension. Equally, it'll be more discriminating and appreciative when it comes to genuinely effective communication.

So your words should have direction, clarity and personality. They should be open and engaging, geared towards the interests of the reader (in this case the customer) rather than the writer. Your writing shouldn't be intimidating; nor should it be patronizing. It should strike balance between informality and stuffiness, chattiness and reserve.

But there are a great many other ways in which your virtual tone of voice needs to be tailored very specifically to the medium. These tips won't turn you into a master. Only practice can do that. But they'll point you on your way, and help you avoid mistakes.

Work out your tone
Tone is the foundation of effective copy. Get this right and you're halfway there. The most important question is, who am I writing this for?

But it's not easy. A helpful trick is to try and build up a picture of your typical customer. Then imagine having a conversation with him or her. What kind of things would you say? What words and phrases would you use (and avoid)? Then try and replicate that in your writing.

One way to develop a successful web tone is to start with your brand. Be clear about the brand values, then think about how these brand values would manifest themselves in the way you write on the web – bearing in mind the need for a more inclusive style anyway.

When you have unpicked the values, try writing some examples of on-brand web copy. Circulate it to others who may have a view. Refine the copy and finally get writing in earnest. You need to be able to answer three questions.

Will the web visitor reading this copy get a sense of what we stand for and believe in? Would they get it from each part of the site, not just the home page? Would they stay, revisit and enjoy the experience?

Give it personality
Closely related to tone is personality. Identifying your customer is one side of the coin. The other is determin-

ing the personality your writing should aim to convey. Put yourself in your customer's shoes, and imagine the kind of person who'd impress him or her. That's your person. He or she has exactly the kind of personality you need in your writing. The bottom line is that each web site, each corporation has a personality whether intentionally expressed or not. Some unfortunately seem to be suffering from multiple personalities. But the web site needs to express your personality.

A company should have a single personality, not several. You wouldn't want a schizoid web site, would you?

So pick out inconsistencies with a fine-tooth comb. This means tone, but also more mundane things. Look, for example, at phrases referring to specific products or services. Are they identical every time? Also look at capital letters, word-size and fonts. Is text spacing consistent? Full-stops, commas, colons?

Trivial, maybe. But someone will notice if you don't get these things right.

Don't over-sell

Chances are that your product won't 'completely transform' your customer's life. Probably it's not even 'amazing!' or 'incredible!' (though hopefully it's good). Nor, in all likelihood, are the savings to be had on it 'unbeatable!'

If you wanted to advertise your qualities as a person (face it – we do it all the time) you'd do it subtly, so it's not too obvious what you're up to. The best web-copy works on other people in a similarly discreet way.

Don't wax lyrical; explain

Business people sometimes see web sites as the ideal opportunity to get out their quill pens and wax lyrical. Resist this (admittedly understandable) impulse.

If people want a literary masterpiece, they'll go to a library. Web writing should be intensely focused on the matter at hand. If it's not completely relevant, it probably needs the red pen.

Make it conversational, but not chatty

Real live people with real live personalities converse, and so should your web site. Conversational writing imitates the tone, diction and cadence of normal speech only with the pauses, stammers and repetitions left out.

Practice by reading out loud what you've written. Does it sound stilted and unnatural? Or does it sound like a real person speaking smoothly and elegantly?

Make it personal

Personal writing is distinct from writing with personality. Making it personal means using pronouns ('you', 'we', 'our', 'your') instead of passive constructions ('can be taken', 'will be done').

Two short samples, one passive, one active.

The 1000th person to visit this site will be sent a free bottle of wine.

We'll send the 1000th person visiting us online a free bottle of wine.

Which has more energy and personality?

Make a strong start

First impressions count – for web sites too. Visuals and functionality matter most for the home page. But after the first click, the words come into their own.

What should that all-important first word-chunk consist of? It doesn't really matter. It could be an 'About us' blurb, it could be a pocket history of the company. But it must be good. Which means accurate, well written and perfectly on-brand.

Be experimental and bold by all means. But don't over-write. Less is more. A good rule of thumb is to write about half as much as you think is needed, then halve it again.

Make it idiosyncratic
While some styles are better than others, no one style is right. Don't be afraid to add a touch of colour to your writing.

True, getting it right means not getting it wrong – that is, avoiding silly mistakes. But it also means writing distinctively and freshly. If your writing is remembered for the right reasons, that means your brand will be remembered for the right reasons too.

There is room for style and zap and unexpected surprises in web writing. The worse web writing is dead on the page. Either too staccato, or too long-winded.

Keep it appropriate
It would be madness to write each part of the web site in the same way. Sometimes people need more information than others. Sometimes on a web page they just need an icon and no words at all. The worst web sites overwhelm with detail at all points. They feel cluttered and poorly thought through. So serious thought and pruning is needed. The watchword must be there should always be sufficient information, but not too much.

Here are some tips:

- Keep the homepage engaging, simple and direct. The words need to quickly capture interest, the design needs to rapidly signal what to do next. A great deal of work needs to go into the words on the homepage; they are after all your shop window, your badge and your flag.

- Keep the very functional pages free from linguistic clutter. If people are transacting with you online then the experience needs to be simple, intuitive and direct. Keep words to a minimum here. Each word must earn its place. Always test these words with users. If the user becomes confused at any point or needs to re-read any sentence then replace the sentence with a clearer, more direct alternative.
- Don't overdo the company information. You don't have to put everything you have ever known about the company and the work you do on the site. Just select enough to be useful and interesting. To bore is to fail.
- Elsewhere be flexible and don't be afraid to experiment.

Write for your site
Keep the type of site you're writing in mind. Is this a site you'll visit for one specific reason? Or is it a portal, somewhere you'll want to spend time looking around?

In the former, lots of copy will simply be a distraction. It needs to be kept to an absolute minimum, performing a simple guiding function and no more. In the latter, the copy will be the main point. So it will more expansive and varied – though consistency, concision and personality should remain firm priorities.

Write less, not more
This can be difficult for many people. But the best writing on the web has a beautiful distilled quality to it. Aim for clarity and precision without becoming too cold and cut back. There is room for style in e-writing but no room for waffle.

Writing for e-commerce needs a great deal of editing. Write a first version, then prune it, then prune it again. The end result is likely to be clearer, more direct e-copy.

Make headings pithy and relevant

Sometimes headings appear to be no more than empty phrases picked at random from the Dictionary of Meaningless Prose. Or else they mean something but don't relate to the text. Or they shout at you – 'Amazing Offer . . . Incredible Savings'.

Good headings draw you into the text that follows. They are unobtrusive but telling. 'About us' is a nice heading. 'All your questions answered' isn't.

The best e-commerce sites use headings to help navigation. If you get too clever with them you'll lose people. The rule of thumb is that headings should easily direct people to what follows.

Think beyond the page

Web pages are not isolated islands. They interconnect logically with each other. Consider a booking process, for example.

Writers should take this into account. Don't slow things down with too much copy. Above all, don't repeat yourself. It's insulting to the customer's intelligence to have the same phrase repeated on three consecutive pages.

Remember that the further in you are, the lighter your copy can become. That way things will seem to go faster, and the customer won't get bored.

Keep sentences short and crisp

Web writing is altogether less leisurely than conventional writing. The Internet is a fast medium, for people with little time on their hands. The aim is not to overwhelm the customer with your old-school eloquence.

Rather it is to impress him or her with how on-the-ball and collected you are.

Web copy shouldn't meander. It should speak clearly, simply and directly. Sentences should be slightly shorter than normal, though not clipped or abrupt.

Avoid jargon and cyberslang

Just because you understand something, that doesn't mean your customer will. Although your copy will make certain assumptions, the rule of thumb on specialist knowledge is to treat your customer as an intelligent ignoramus. So avoid business jargon ('processed') and cyberslang (hot-button). Everyone will be grateful (including your fellow experts). And don't assume that spelling something out clearly is the same as being patronizing – it isn't.

Don't spell out what's obvious

Sometimes you come across the following:

> To return to the homepage, click on go to homepage
> *go to homepage*

It doesn't take a genius to see there's something wrong here. The problem is the instructing mentality, which holds that if the customer is going to do something, first it must be spelt out. Wrong. Web sites aren't like that. It's the customer doing the instructing. They'll know what to do or at the least the functionality should be so good they don't need telling and double telling what to do.

Use plain, simple words where possible

Long or complex words make your writing cumbersome, heavy, indigestible. Whereas plain ones make it natural and engaging. This doesn't mean writing for the lowest common denominator. Instead it means always preferring simplicity over complexity. Always making the e-commerce experience as easy and straightforward as possible. And never waste people's precious time.

Don't be abrupt

Good web writing has colour and texture and personality. The best text is light and a pleasure to read. While we aim to keep words to a minimum, effective e-writing is never abrupt. This becomes especially true in sites that are content rich and aim for prolonged stickiness.

In sites that aim to create a sense of community or common interest (often called portals) part of the appeal is style and a sense of belonging. Abruptness here simply seems to denote a lack of interest.

E-commerce is after all one great buying conversation and who wants to buy from someone who is rude and abrupt?

Don't try and be too cool

Everyone knows that the Internet is a hip medium. But that doesn't mean your website should try too hard to be cool.

Remember, really cool people are usually cool not because of what they say, but because of what they don't say. I am not advocating that your site should have the personality of Clint Eastwood. But nor should it be too chatty and in-your-face. Get the balance right between personality and reserve, calm and enthusiasm. Don't shout, talk. Don't shuffle, stroll.

There is starting to be some clear evidence that many traditional companies are running very effective sites using relatively traditional language. Just because the internet seems hip and trendy now this will not always be the case. As everyone gets access to the web and every company has a site, then it will seem normal. When this happens, traditional companies with a grafted-on hip style will seem frankly ridiculous.

Avoid Cliché

Clichés are hard to define, but their basic meaning is any word or phrase that is over-used. In copy-writing, 'valued customer' is a good example of a cliché. So is 'making your life easier'. These were probably good phrases once. Now they've been killed by over-use.

The general rule (sadly) is: if something comes to you quickly, it's probably clichéd. Why? Because it will already be in your brain. To write freshly is to create anew every time. But it takes time and effort – don't think it's easy.

The worst kind of cliché comes from the direct mail industry: *simply fill in, bargain offer, completely free* and so on. Avoid this at all cost. It is a pollution on the web. The web is a conversation and this kind of hyped-up language looks madly out of place. If you spoke in the clichés of the direct mail world you wouldn't have many friends. And on the web, nor would your business.

To *sum up*

So what makes great language for e-commerce? At the basic level it needs to be appropriate. The web is inter-active, fast and accessible, so the language used must reflect these qualities.

But we are not saying that all e-language needs to be the same. Any e-copy needs to have personality and style, needs to be carefully distilled and crafted.

As with any business writing, e-copy needs to be fit for the purpose. It needs to be what your users want, not what you want to present. It is hard to be very prescriptive about the new language of e-commerce but there are some simple tips that are worth bearing in mind.

- Always try to keep your **writing clear and direct**. People have enormous choice on the Internet and are not afraid to use it. If you waffle or present stodgy copy then the chances are the user will try a more engaging site.
- Develop **a web personality and stick to it**. Make sure the personality is real for you. Be clear about it and develop a style and tone to match. The really sticky sites (sites people stay with and come back to) have a great sense of personality and a consistent one too.
- Remember **functionality, design and words all have weight**. They back each other up. Functionality without an effective tone is a wasted opportunity.
- **Be modern**. Very traditional bureaucratic copy is not appropriate. The web is a modern medium and it requires the language of modern business to match. This means it's fine to start a sentence with 'And', to use contractions and to use active verbs.
- **Be inclusive**. Welcome interactivity but don't be high-handed. Avoid hype and fluff and the language of the brochure and direct mail. It will only alienate surfers. E-commerce is a global conversation and we need a language that fits all. Don't be too ironic if you want to appeal to a wider audience.

A FINAL WORD

As we look ahead into the new century, just what are the millions of networked computers, humming away on the Internet, achieving? High on the list is that they free us from the drudgeries of life. At work, the dull functions of office life are being liquidated: filing, searching of records, processing orders, counting the money, all are now possible at the press of a button. We can work from home, even on the move.

On the individual level, installations in the home mean that young mothers can return to the work market. Shopping can be done without leaving the front door, the whole gamut of human knowledge is at our fingertips, mankind is being linked up as never before.

But perhaps time is the new technology's greatest gift. By relieving us of the drudgery it gives us time to think about our businesses, to develop ourselves as human beings, time to devote to our families.

And yet it is still a moving world, with new developments, new horizons, coming with bewildering speed. Experts say they are unsure about the future. Nobody knows just how far technology will change business and society, but everyone knows it will.

There is no time to teach, and nowhere else to learn. So jump in!

THE PERFECT PRESENTATION

Andrew Leigh and Michael Maynard

Many people are terrified of making a presentation in public, while others are just unsure of how to go about it effectively. But the ability to do it successfully can make all the difference to your personal career, and to the business prospects of your firm. This book provides a sure-fire method based on the 5 Ps of Perfect Presentation: Preparation, Purpose, Presence, Passion and Personality. It is an excellent, hands-on guide which takes the reader step by step to success in one of the most important business skills.

£6.99   0 09 941002 8

PERFECT NEGOTIATION

Gavin Kennedy

The ability to negotiate effectively is a vital skill required in business and everyday situations.

Whether you are negotiating over a business deal, a pay rise, a difference of opinion between managers and staff, or the price of a new house or car, this invaluable book, written by one of Europe's leading experts in negotiation, will help you to get a better deal every time, and avoid costly mistakes.

£6.99   0 09 941016 8

PERFECT TIME MANAGEMENT

Edward Johns

Managing your time effectively means adding value to everything you do. This book will help you to master the techniques and skills essential to grasping control of your time and your life.

If you can cut down the time you spend meeting people, talking on the phone, writing and reading business papers and answering subordinates' questions, you can use the time saved for creative work and the really important elements of your job. Learn how to deal with interruptions, manage the cost and cut down on meetings time – above all, how to minimize paperwork. You'll be amazed how following a few simple guidelines will improve the quality of both your working life and your leisure time.

£6.99   0 09 941004 4

THE PERFECT BUSINESS PLAN

Ron Johnson

A really professional business plan is crucial to success. This book provides a planning framework and shows you how to complete it for your own business in 100 easy to follow stages.

Business planning will help you to make better decisions today, taking into account as many of the relevant factors as possible. A carefully prepared business plan is essential to the people who will put money into the business, to those who will lend it money, and above all to the people who carry out its day to day management.

£6.99   0 09 941005 2

PERFECT ASSERTIVENESS

Jan Ferguson

Perfect Assertiveness helps you to understand more about assertiveness and its importance as a life skill. The book shows you the difference between assertiveness and aggression, and teaches you to understand more about yourself, the possibilities of change and the potential for improvement in personal, social, family and workplace relationships.

£6.99   0 09 940617 9